To Ένυπνιον. [Translated by Ch. A. Parmenides. Originally published in "The Prisoner of Chillon, and other poems."]

George Byron

To Ἐνυπνιον. [Translated by Ch. A. Parmenides. Originally published in "The Prisoner of Chillon, and other poems."]
Byron, George
British Library, Historical Print Editions
British Library
11779.c.29.

The BiblioLife Network

This project was made possible in part by the BiblioLife Network (BLN), a project aimed at addressing some of the huge challenges facing book preservationists around the world. The BLN includes libraries, library networks, archives, subject matter experts, online communities and library service providers. We believe every book ever published should be available as a high-quality print reproduction; printed on- demand anywhere in the world. This insures the ongoing accessibility of the content and helps generate sustainable revenue for the libraries and organizations that work to preserve these important materials.

The following book is in the "public domain" and represents an authentic reproduction of the text as printed by the original publisher. While we have attempted to accurately maintain the integrity of the original work, there are sometimes problems with the original book or micro-film from which the books were digitized. This can result in minor errors in reproduction. Possible imperfections include missing and blurred pages, poor pictures, markings and other reproduction issues beyond our control. Because this work is culturally important, we have made it available as part of our commitment to protecting, preserving, and promoting the world's literature.

GUIDE TO FOLD-OUTS, MAPS and OVERSIZED IMAGES

In an online database, page images do not need to conform to the size restrictions found in a printed book. When converting these images back into a printed bound book, the page sizes are standardized in ways that maintain the detail of the original. For large images, such as fold-out maps, the original page image is split into two or more pages.

Guidelines used to determine the split of oversize pages:

- Some images are split vertically; large images require vertical and horizontal splits.
- For horizontal splits, the content is split left to right.
- For vertical splits, the content is split from top to bottom.
- For both vertical and horizontal splits, the image is processed from top left to bottom right.

SOLD for THE PRINCE OF WALES'S
NATIONAL RELIEF FUND

EIGHT **The Guinea Doll** PENCE

NET.

A STORY BOOK OF RHYMES FOR CHILDREN
ARRANGED AS A PLAY FOR AMATEURS
WITH PHOTOGRAPHS OF TOYS

1914

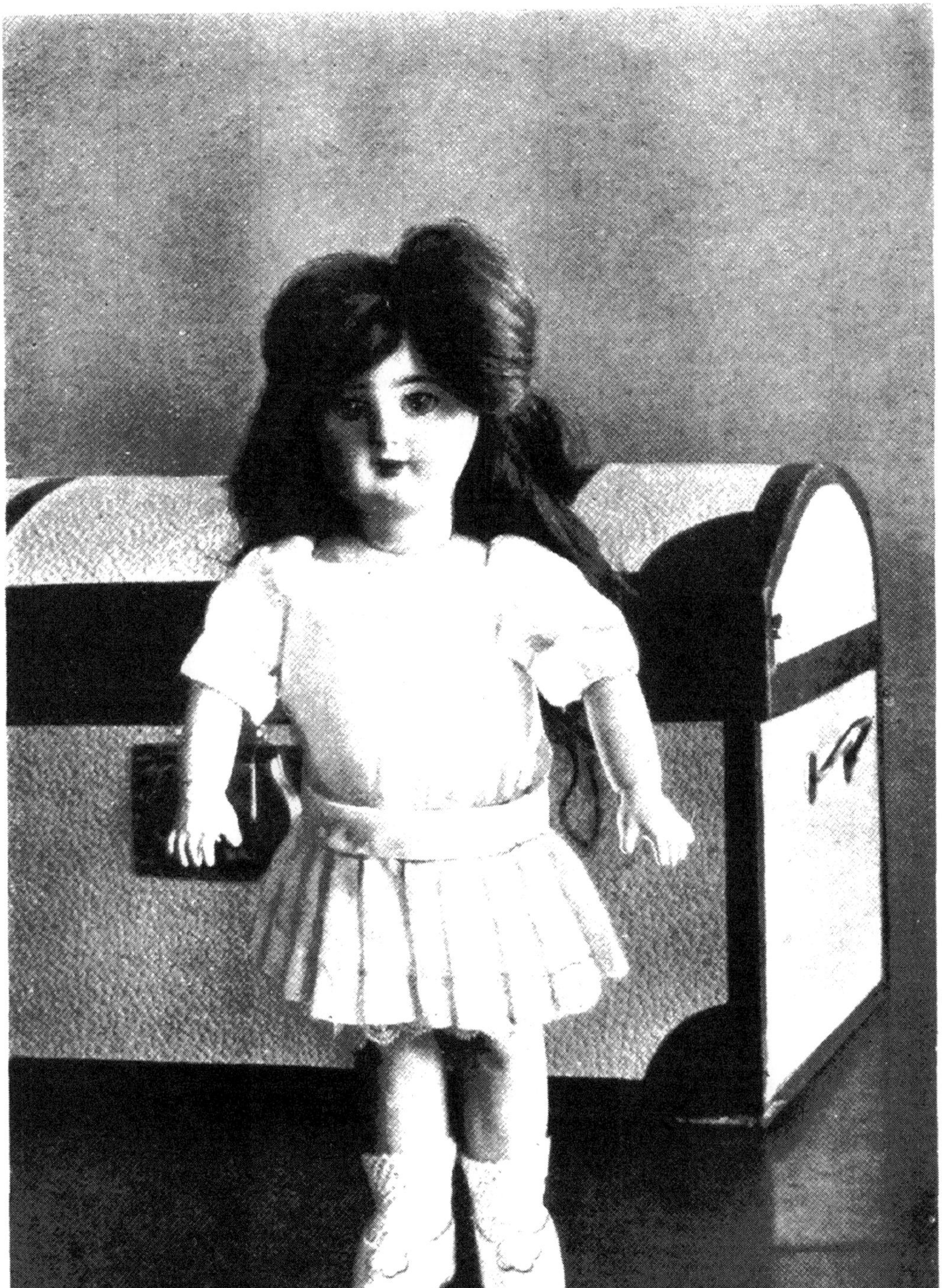

FOR THE PRINCE OF WALES'S
NATIONAL RELIEF FUND

THE GUINEA DOLL

By FLORA MARONE

A STORY WRITTEN AS A PLAY FOR
AMATEURS, IN RHYMES,
FOR CHILDREN

LONDON
THE SAINT CATHERINE PRESS
34 NORFOLK ST · STRAND
W.C.

THE GUINEA DOLL

(In 4 Acts.)

One scene the entire piece—The Toyroom Upstairs.

ACT I.

1. Dame Trot introduces The Guinea One.
2. Cupid introduces himself.
3. Dame Trot calls in Three Little Boys, who march with guns and sing a song.
4. The Guinea One brings in The Aero Cat.
5. Dame Trot claims The Aero Cat and runs away with it.

End of Act I.

ACT II.

1. Three Fairies, The Guinea One and Dame Trot.
2. Fairy Kindheart receives the packet.
3. The Guinea One watches Dame Trot play cards; they both recite rhymes.
4. Cupid again, he finds the red heart.
5. Gaddy enters and The Guinea One enters.

6. Gaddy's rhymes.

7. Gaddy asks the animals to come upstairs.

8. Gaddy then Cupid, The Guinea One and Dame Trot.

End of Act II.

ACT III.

1. The Toad appears.
2. The Aero Cat appears as Zulu with Blanche.

End of Act III.

ACT IV.

1. Cupid hangs up mistletoe. The Fairy finds her damaged heart.

2. Cupid laughs at The Fairy, who puts on her heart again.

3. Enter Fleetfoot and Moneybags; they talk with Kindheart.

4. Enter The Pudding.

5. The Guinea One tries to find a stocking for Santa Claus. Chorus behind stage.

6. The Supper Table and Cupid, etc.

7. Three Little Boys sing the National Anthem.

THE END.

CHARACTERS

(Supposed to be all Toys)

THE GUINEA DOLL: *In white.*

DAME TROT: *Dark red skirt, blue check or plaid scarf round shoulders which ties at back in a large knot; brown paper hat, white frilled cap.*

CUPID: *In white, with small wings.*

GADDY: *In white tissue paper dress, with muslin lining to prevent tearing. Brown paper hat, paper roses, pink.*

THE AERO CAT: *A black toy.*

ZULU (*The Aero Cat again*): *A Boy in a Cat Mask, black.*

BLANCHE: *A girl in a white Cat Mask.*

TOAD: *A toy, or a boy in a Toad Mask.*

PUDDING: *Boy in a brown mask.*

THREE LITTLE BRITISH BOYS: *To march and sing, either dressed as Highlanders, Jack Tars, or Boy Scouts, or one of each.*

THREE CHRISTMAS FAIRIES: *Irish, Scotch and English.*

KINDHEART (*an Irish Fairy*): *In white dress, rather short small wings, three rows of red ribbon on skirt the same colour as red heart, a red sash band.*

The Red Heart should be 6 inches long. Green ribbon on hair tied at back; some shamrock leaves on the green ribbon. Red shoes look nicer than white or black.

FLEETFOOT (*a Scotch Fairy*): *In white dress, small wings, three rows of blue ribbon on skirt and waist, a long blue stocking in hand—can be made of any material. Some green thistles with blue tops worn round head on a piece of green ribbon tied at back. Shoes blue.*

MONEYBAGS (*an English Fairy*): *In white dress, small wings, yellow ribbon on skirt and round waist, white roses on green ribbon round head, carries a yellow Bag with the word Money on it.*

THE STAGE
ONLY ONE SCENE · NO CURTAIN NECESSARY

Procure some bamboo canes, 10 feet or 7 or 8 feet high, or wooden poles, tie each firmly to a chair back.

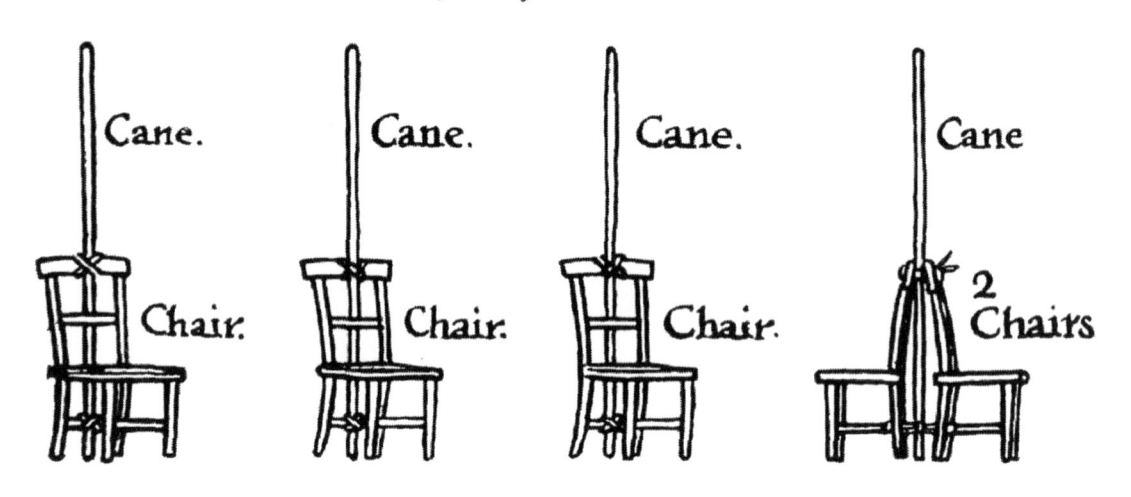

Cane. Chair. Cane. Chair. Cane. Chair. Cane 2 Chairs

Borrow some white sheets, join them together with needle and cotton, sew on strong tapes at the tops. Tie them to the rods or canes. You now have a plain background. All you have to do is to decorate it with red and blue ribbons or muslins and loop up with white paper rosettes.

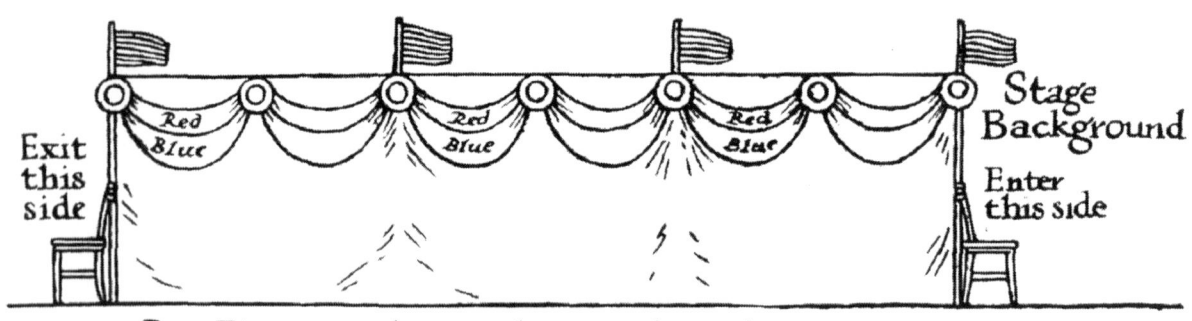

Exit this side — Red Blue — Red Blue — Red Blue — Stage Background Enter this side

Put Flags on the top but nothing heavy

FLAGS NAVAL — TO DECORATE THE STAGE

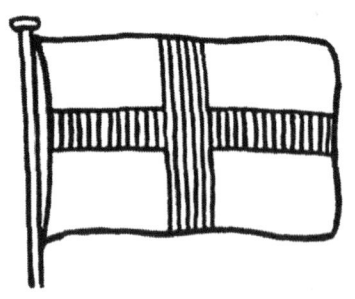

BRITISH. Union Jack.

ENGLISH. St George's Cross.
White ground with red cross.

SCOTCH. St Andrew's Cross.
A blue ground and white cross corner to corner.

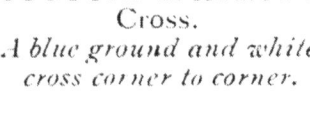

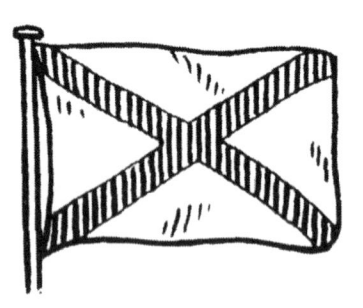

IRISH. St Patrick's Cross.
White ground with red cross corner to corner.

BELGIAN FLAG.
Green, yellow, red.

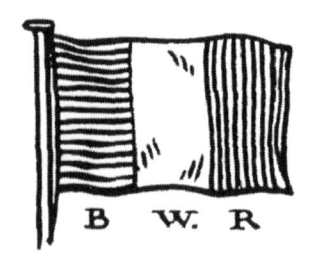

FRENCH FLAG.
Blue, white, red.

RUSSIAN (Naval).
White ground, blue cross corner to corner.

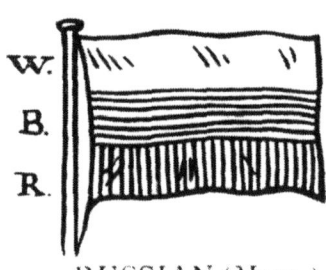

RUSSIAN (Merc.)
White, blue, red.

THE GUINEA DOLL

One Scene throughout the play—THE TOYROOM UPSTAIRS.

ACT I.

Enter DAME TROT *and* THE GUINEA DOLL.

DAME TROT *introduces* THE GUINEA ONE *as follows:*—

> When first she came she stood and gazed
> On us a stranger shy and dazed;
> Her trunk the smartest I have seen
> Was worthy of a little queen;
> Well, as the newness goes now she
> Will soon be happy as can be;
> For here upstairs she'll meet so many,
> Some worth a lot, some worth a penny.
>
> *Exeunt* DAME TROT.

[*The trunk need not be seen in the play.*]

Enter CUPID, *speaking to* GUINEA ONE.

> How do you do,
>   I'm Cupid Boy.
> And you are new,
>   The guinea toy;
> It would arrive,
>   A doll, I heard;
> You look alive,
>   Upon my word.

>   And can you shoot?
>   Because now I
>   To teach you that
>   Fine sport will try.
>   I'm noted for my shooting skill
>   The whole world over. I can drill
>   You gradually
>   From day to day,
>   If only you have
>   Come to stay.
>   *Exeunt* CUPID *and* GUINEA ONE.

Enter DAME TROT.
>   I heard him talk of skilful shot,
>   Just see the little men I've got.
>   Come forward Sandy, Pat and Bill,
>   And show the people how *you* drill.
>   These bonnie laddies shoot with guns,
>   Sometimes with very heavy ones.

THREE LITTLE BOYS *come in, march round, keeping step, dressed in uniform. They sing a song to the piano [something patriotic].*

>   *Exeunt* THREE LITTLE BOYS.

Enter THE GUINEA ONE *holding* THE AERO CAT.

THE GUINEA ONE, *as she puts it on the ground:*
>   This dropp'd out of an aeroplane,
>   It fell upon the ground;
>   You can imagine we were vain
>   To find it safe and sound.

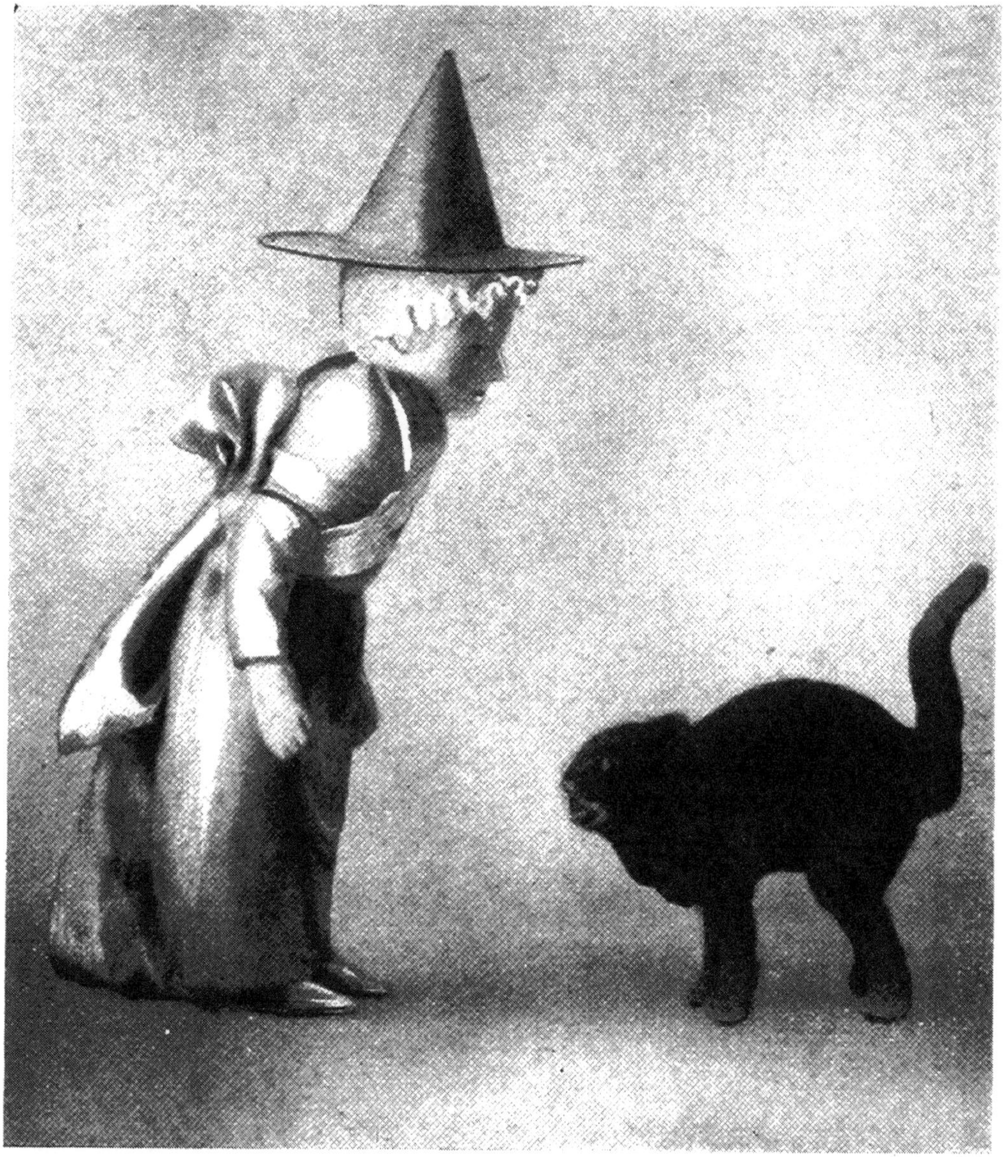

But just at first we were so scared
    We took it for a bomb;
It came so rapidly, it fared
    Remarkably this Tom.

Alighting firm, not hurt a bit
    Like any other cat;
It can stand tiptoe, it can sit,
    Or sleep, upon the mat.

But when it purrs—oh, Dratt!
It makes you certain that
It's more than just a lucky cat,
It is an Aero Cat.

NOTE. *Here if possible let the sound of a motor be heard behind the scenes or outside the window.*

Enter DAME TROT—GUINEA ONE *looking on.*

I am the old woman
    Who owned a nice cat;
It was but a kitten,
    Whose creature is that?
The lost one of mine
    Was smaller and thinner;
Put in a show would have
    Been a good winner.
My cat went away.

>   For weeks I suppose it
>   Grew up in that time,
>   Now nobody knows it.
>   I've stood by my door
>   With so doleful a ditty,
>   And cried " Little cat,
>   Oh, come back, little kitty! "
>   I am the old woman
>   Who called it and said,
>   " If kitten won't come
>   Let this cat come instead."

She picks it up and runs away with it.

Enter THREE FAIRIES—*They sit together in the middle of stage,* GUINEA DOLL *one side,* DAME *on the other.*

MONEYBAGS: Three Fairies flown from Fairyland
She sees us sitting hand in hand,
And she is quite amused to hear
So much about when we appear—

FLEETFOOT: as Fleetfoot,

KINDHEART: Kindheart,

MONEYBAGS: Moneybags.

FLEETFOOT: On many things her chatter wags;
Yes, Christmas time and all the cheer
It brings to children far and near.

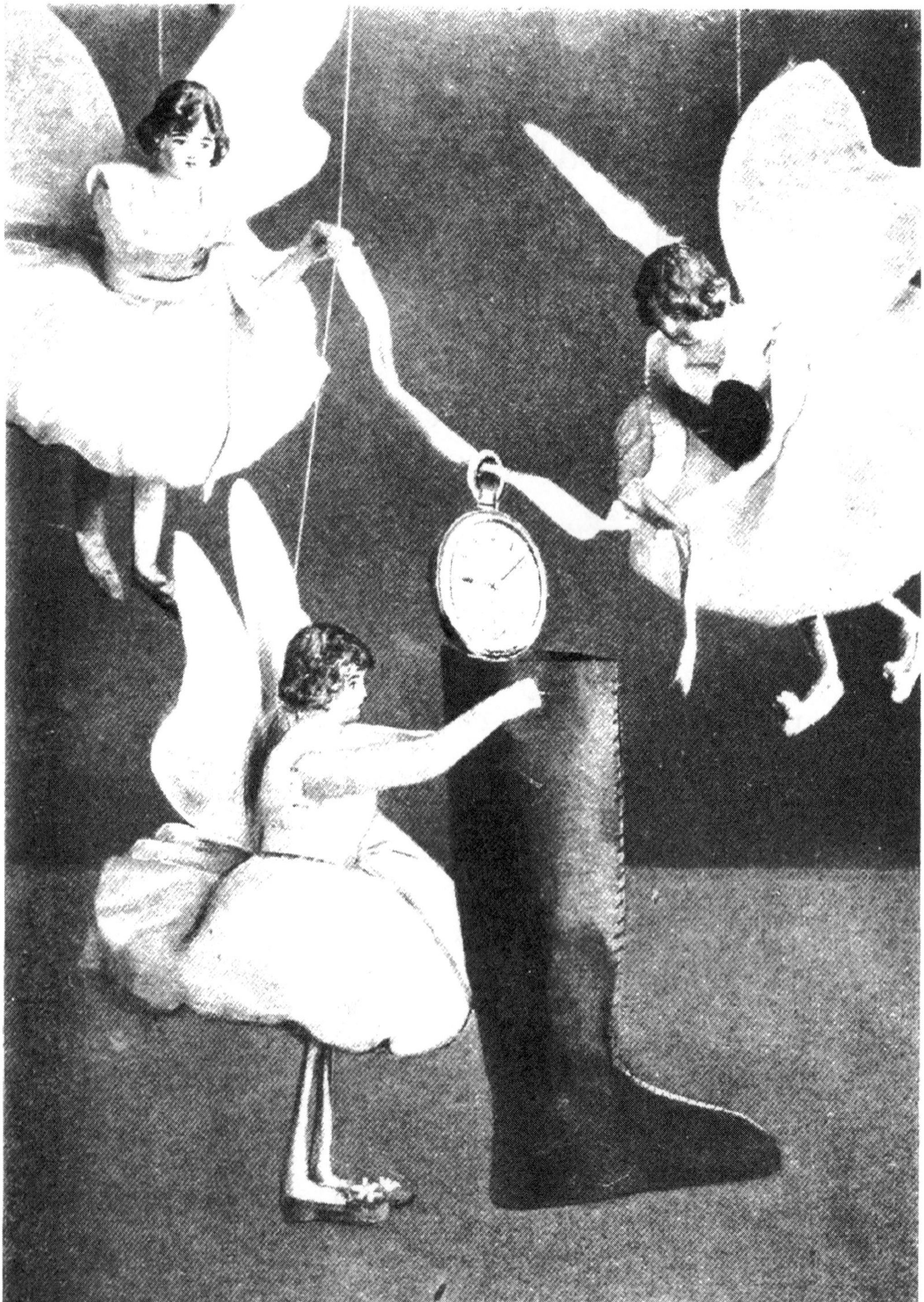

MONEYBAGS: How we with Santa Claus must choose
What shall be put in socks and shoes.

KINDHEART: When Fleetfoot Fairy pausing, said,
A naughty girl who is in bed,
Has been so very bad this year
She won't get anything, I fear.

MONEYBAGS *(speaking)*: The Guinea Doll was much disturbed
This dreadful verdict to have heard.

FLEETFOOT: She said, I hope 'tis but in fun
You say this, let her have just one;
Just one thing let her.

MONEYBAGS: It's so sad
Her disappointment
Though she's bad.

GUINEA ONE: I shouldn't like to have nothing this year.

DAME TROT: Some little children won't get much, I fear.

DAME TROT *now speaks of the war, of the poor little children in Belgium, France and Russia who have lost their fathers, if not their homes, and about ourselves, and anything in the newspaper at the time.*

Exeunt GUINEA ONE *and* DAME TROT.
Exeunt FLEETFOOT, *leaving the Fairies,*
MONEYBAGS *and* KINDHEART *still sitting on the stage.*

Enter FLEETFOOT, *bearing a packet. This she hands to* KINDHEART, *saying*:
"The Post."

FLEETFOOT *retires.*

KINDHEART *unties the packet and finds a large heart inside. She shows it to* MONEYBAGS.

MONEYBAGS *remarks:*
>The Fairy Kindheart,
>   Would you think it?
>Has just received
>   This pretty trinket.

KINDHEART: A lovely heart of beads,
      All red.
   And with it too the
      Letter said.

Scanning it quickly:
   Do read it, Moneybags.

MONEYBAGS, *reading aloud:*
>   Dear Fairy Kindheart (*pause*)
>   Years ago
>   You always sent me
>   Things, I know.
>   Just what I wanted
>   Most I got;
>   And in my stocking
>   Such a lot.

22

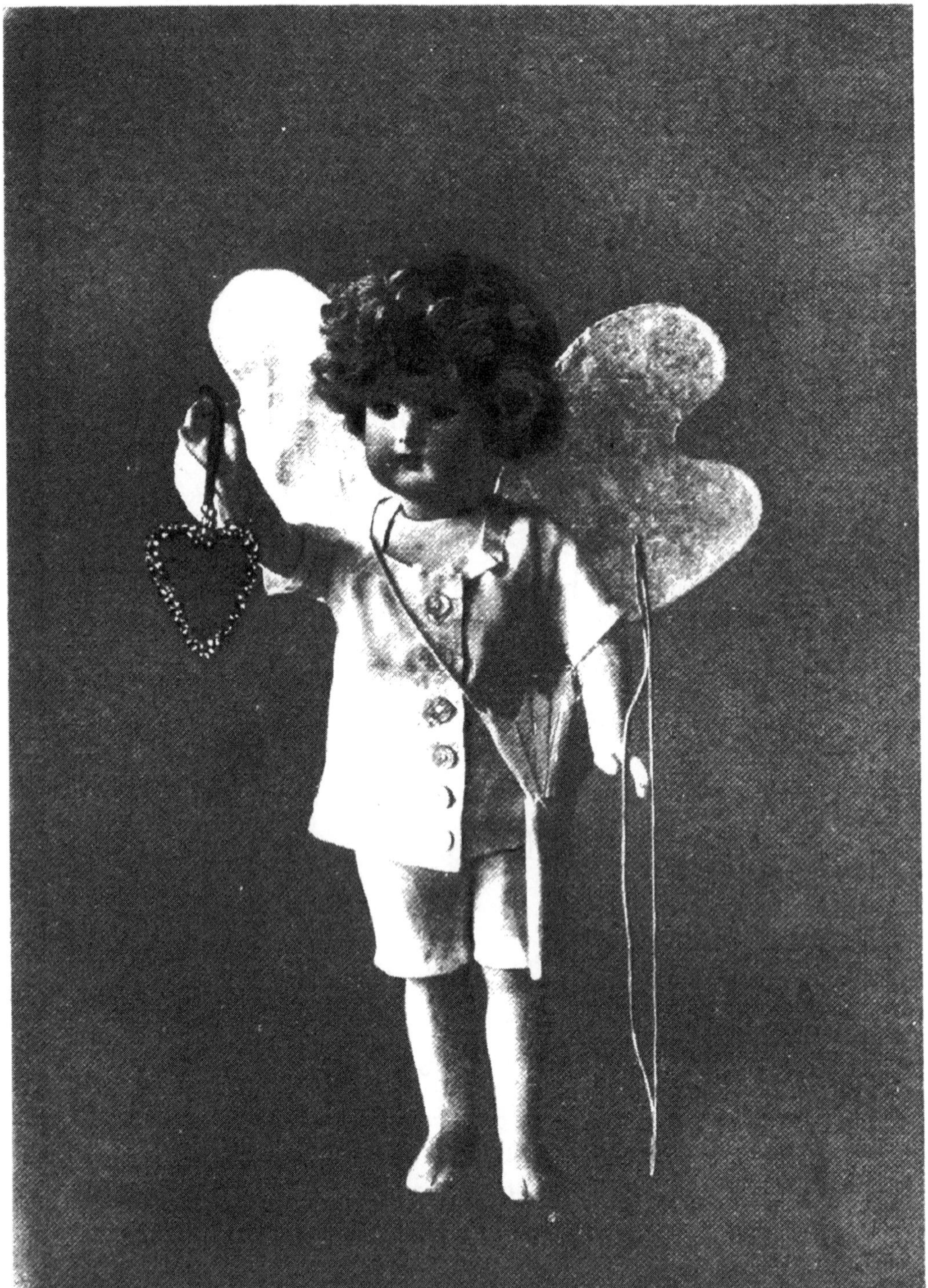

  Then I was small,
    Now I have grown;
  I made this heart
    For you alone.
   For all your kindness
    In the past.
  And when this reaches you, at last,
  Do wear it, Fairy, round your neck,
  Where you would choose, your dress to deck
  At gaieties where you take part,
  Be sure you wear my red, red heart.

  Come, Fairy, take it from its paper,
  And put it on, we'll dance a caper.
        Both dance away.
  Exeunt KINDHEART *and* MONEYBAGS, *dancing.*

Enter GUINEA ONE *from one side with cat.*

Enter DAME TROT *from other side with a pack of cards. Both seat themselves at a small table opposite to one another. The* GUINEA ONE *puts the cat on the table. The old woman plays a game of cards, " Old Maid," entirely herself, dealing them in two heaps. The* GUINEA ONE *is only allowed to watch the game and stroke the cat.*

If there is not much room on the stage the old woman should bring her table in with her and take it out again when she goes.

The GUINEA ONE, *watching the game, recites a rhyme.*

GUINEA ONE: My trunk is my fortune,

DAME TROT: The Guinea One said;

GUINEA ONE: I'm keeping it nice
    Till the day I am wed.
A bevy of maidens
    Shall hold up my train;
I'll step out beside him,
    I hope it won't rain.

DAME TROT: To step out beside him,
    I hope it won't rain.

GUINEA ONE: I shall really look smart,
    All dressed out in white;
The folks they will stare
    At the beautiful sight.
To see it before me
    I shut my eyes tight.

The old woman still goes on playing cards in silence, the GUINEA ONE *watching.*

The GUINEA ONE, *still watching the game, begins another rhyme:*

GUINEA ONE: When the old lady sat
    All alone with her cat,
Playing cards, and her hat
    Had a brim very flat.

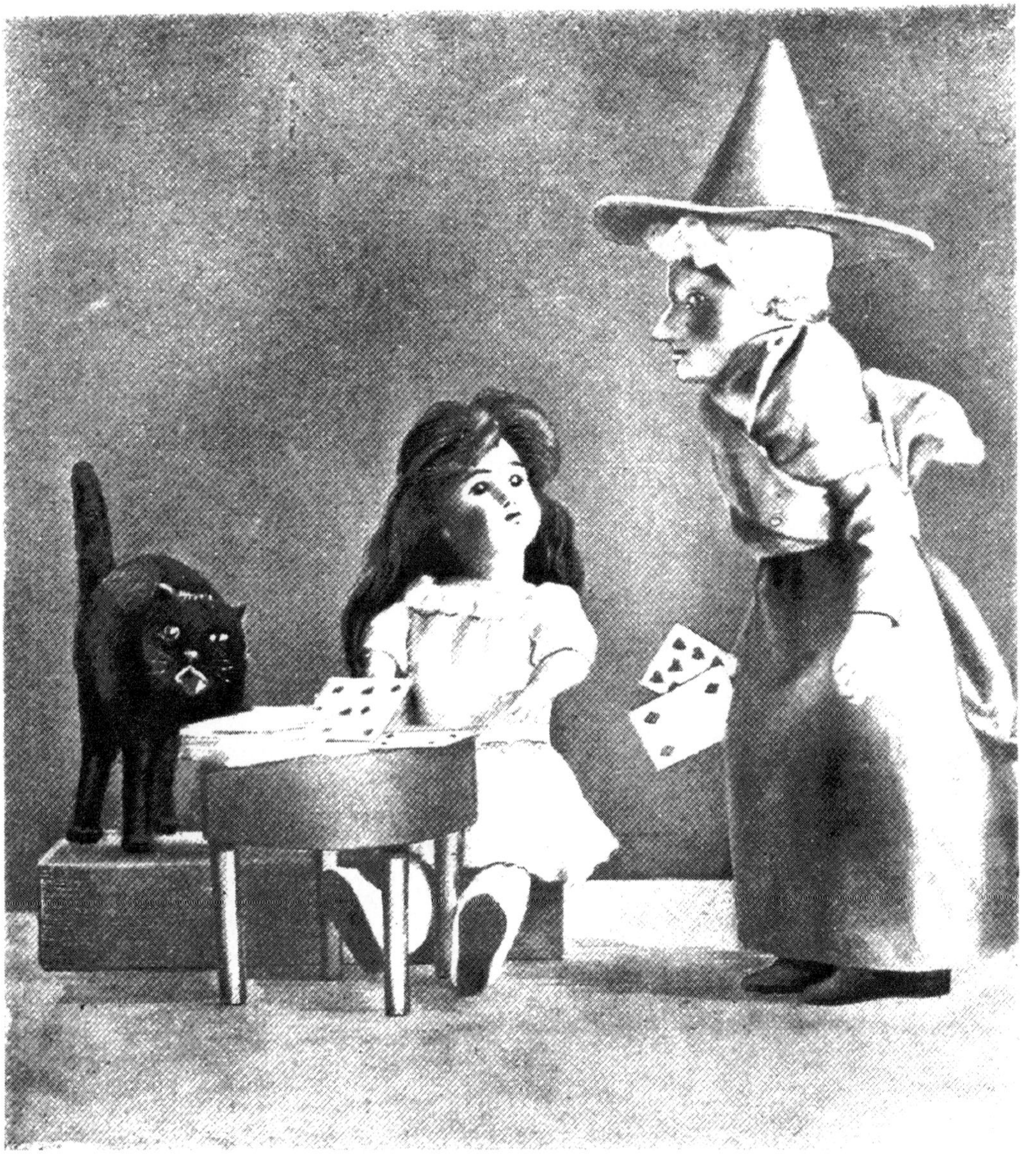

DAME TROT: Then she asked me the name
Of my wonderful game;
Would I teach her the same,
For that reason she came.

GUINEA ONE: And I felt very gay
When I got her to say,
" I will show you the way
If you sit down and play."

DAME TROT: As my last card I laid
On the top with her spade
In a gruff voice I said
" You will be an old maid."

DAME TROT *picks up her cards.*

GUINEA ONE *follows with the cat. Exeunt.*

Enter CUPID. *The heart should be somewhere on the ground.*

They say I've been a nuisance
Ever since I came,
Pulling Fairy ringlets
When I join their game.
Pranks I've played so many,
Cry they, " 'Tis a shame,
Slippers missing, know we
Cupid is to blame."

What is this that sparkles,
    Heart upon the ground;
Look, I say, how funny,
    Look at what I've found.
Heart as red as cherries ripe,
    Beads on wire bound;
Anybody want it,
    Chase me for it round.

Enter GUINEA ONE, *who chases him for it. They both disappear, heart and all.*

Enter GADDY, *singing:*
    The sun it cannot get at me
    When I'm away from bush and tree,
        In the garden,
        The beautiful garden.

    Because my hat is large and round,
    With paper roses, too, it's crowned,
        In the garden,
        The beautiful garden.

GADDY *wears a white paper dress, brown paper hat with pink roses and green leaves.*

Enter the GUINEA ONE, *looking at* GADDY. *She says to her,* "Who are you?" GADDY *answers sweetly,* "I'm Gaddy," *adding to the audience—*
    I've just come up from the garden,
        It is so beautiful down there;
    I shall never, never pardon
        You, if you really do not care.

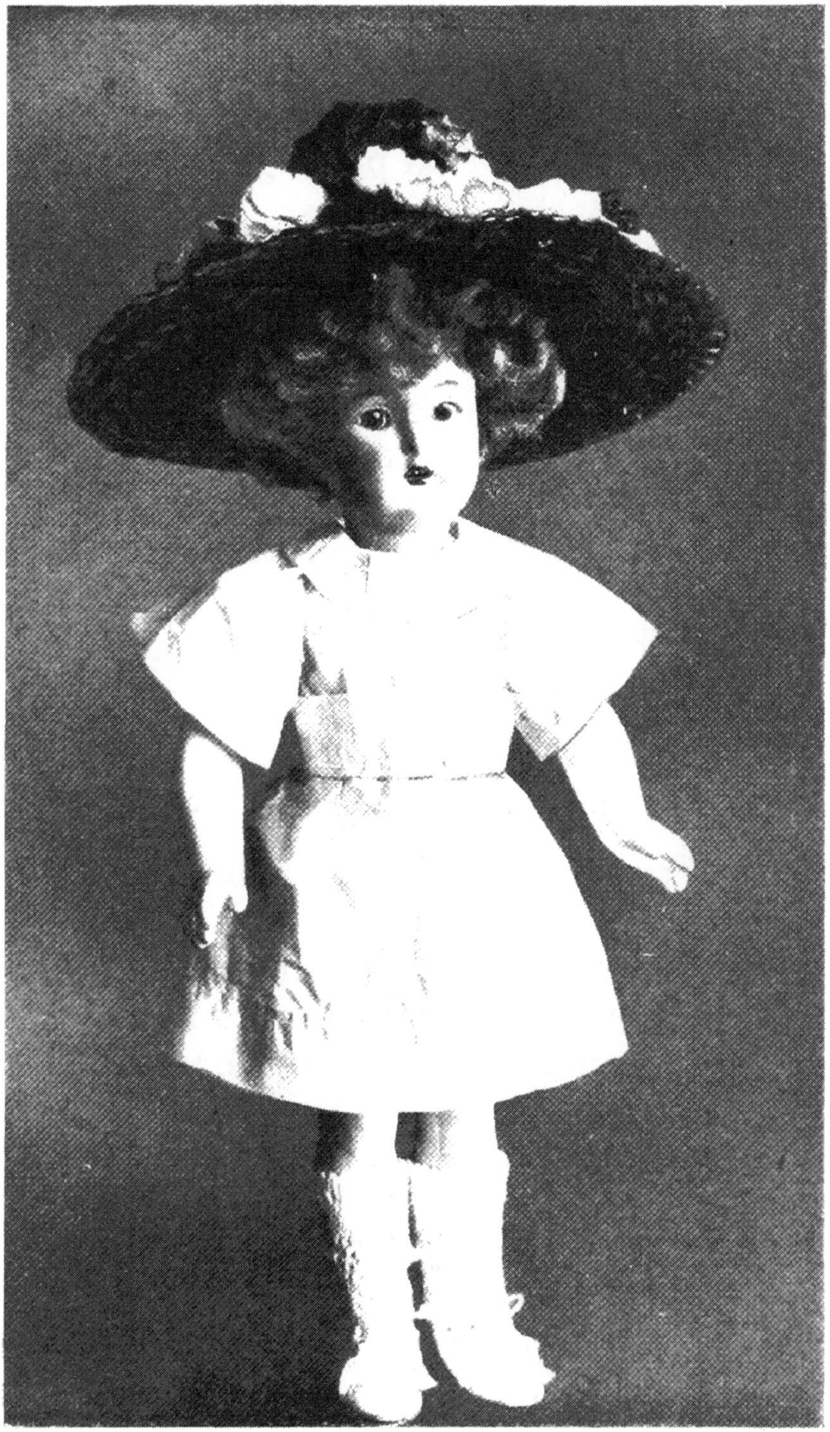

For roses and trees and thrushes,
    And such a dear old ugly toad;
While further off there rushes
    Some motor car passing the road.

The GUINEA ONE: " But who are you really? "
GADDY, *sweetly:* " I'm Gaddy."

GADDY: I've something funny to relate,
A thing of interest to state;
My clothes I always wear of paper
Now that makes you stare a gaper.

Child, never mind, I'll say my rhymes,
I've often said them, times and times.

GADDY'S RHYMES.

Young Gaddy was a little girl
Who nicely kept her hair in curl,
Who always dressed in paper frocks,
Wore paper in her shoes and socks.
'Twas awkward when she tore her clothes,
Which often happened I suppose;
Then she would have indoors to stay
Till she got more, I've heard her say.
Once every week she dressed in new,
Sometimes a pink, sometimes a blue;
Or maybe green or yellow shade,
So changed about this giddy maid.

GADDY: Come down into the garden, Guinea One.

GUINEA ONE: I don't know if I might.

GADDY: I never trouble about if I might or not; I always do what I like.

GUINEA ONE: I'm afraid you are a naughty girl. I know who you are; you are the bad girl who is to get nothing this Christmas; the fairies told me.

GADDY *laughs immoderately at this: it amuses her very much indeed.*

GADDY: Come down into the garden, Guinea One.

GUINEA ONE: No, I won't; can't you bring some of it up here?

GADDY: I will try, Guinea One. There is the old thrush, Guinea One.

GUINEA ONE: Bring it up.

GADDY: There is the old Toad.

GUINEA ONE: Bring it up.

GADDY: There is the White Cat and the Black Cat.

GUINEA ONE: Bring them up.

GADDY: I'll try, Guinea One. I'll hear what they say.
         GADDY *retires, smiling.*

GUINEA ONE: I do hope she will bring them all up.

Gaddy *enters.*

          I asked them to
             Come up the stair
          For coming down
             You did not care.
          The Toad, he said
             He'd think about it;
          That you were wise
             He did not doubt it.
          The Thrush, he said
             He never would
          Come up and stare,
             Not if he could.
          The Black Cat said
             He'd often done it,
          There was no reason
             He should shun it.
          The Cat all white
             She said that she,
          To come upstairs
             Did quite agree.

Guinea One: That's very good of them. All but the Thrush he says he won't come up.

Gaddy: Yes, and he's such a fine fellow; only yesterday, down in the beautiful garden—
          Yesterday that Thrush, gay bird,
             Shouted from the tallest tree,
          Sounding so much when I heard,
             Like one beckoning in glee;

>Like Gaddy with the dark brown hair.
>   Like Gaddy with the slippers neat.
> Come out to the orchard there,
>   Where the apples smell so sweet.
> Apples falling at your feet,
>   Autumn cheerful as in May;
> Gaddy with the slippers neat
>   Come out near the trees and play.

GADDY: Where are the scissors?—*throwing her hat away across the stage.*

GUINEA ONE: Here they are.

GADDY *takes them and tears his frock right down the front and steps out of it. It is* CUPID *without his wings.*

CUPID: You asked me who I was? I'm Cupid.

GUINEA ONE *cries and says:* Oh, what a take in!

Enter DAME TROT: What's the matter, Guinea One? Don't cry.

GUINEA ONE: I've lost Gaddy.

DAME TROT: Won't that little boy do to play with.

GUINEA ONE: No, I've lost Gaddy altogether.

CUPID: Don't cry, Guinea One; remember they're coming upstairs.

GUINEA ONE *brightens up at once:* Oh, yes, I remember.

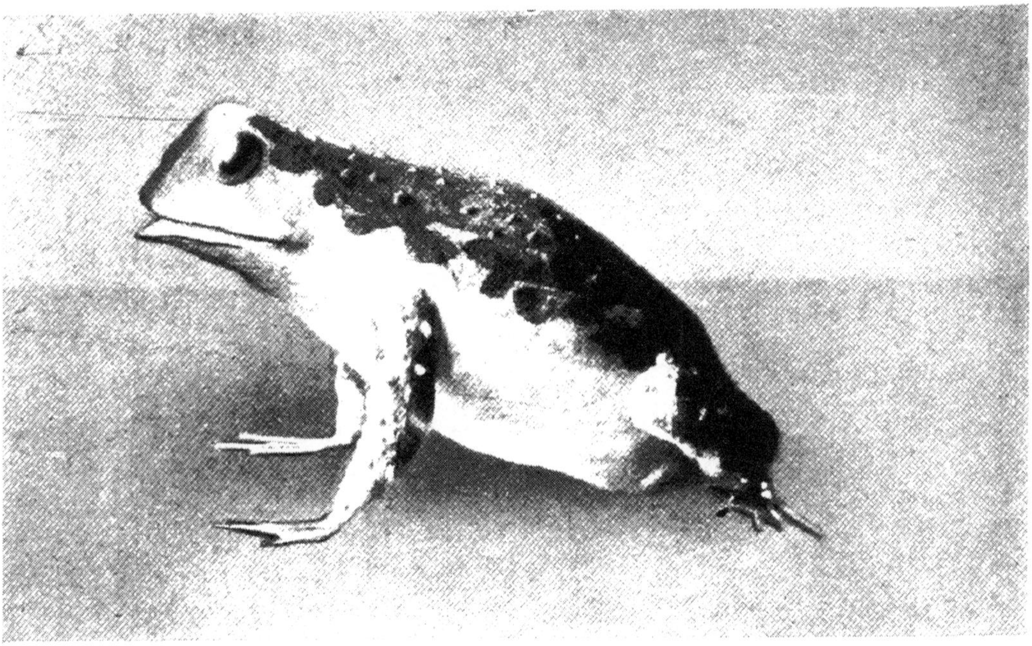

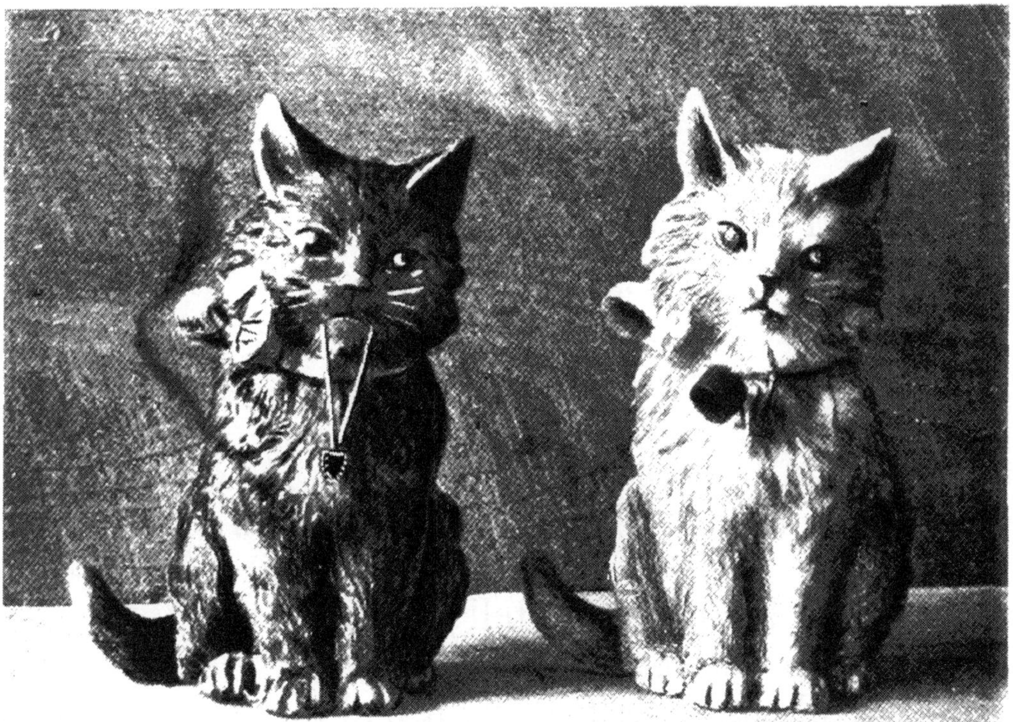

Enter THE TOAD—*his rhymes:*

I am the big Toad, who made his abode
        Inside of a rut
        Of the water-butt,
Which, trigged upon brick, was solid and thick.
        When seasons were hot
        No water it got.
But oft in the rain, quite over there came
A flood down the side, and big puddles wide;
        The earth was squashy,
        Miry and sloshy.
And this I did find all quite to my mind;
For what do I care, when down my hole there
        I hide under ground,
        I sleep so profound.

ZULU AND BLANCHE
THE BLACK CAT, THE WHITE CAT.

My name is Zulu, I am black,
Of late I do not heed the clack
Of other cats; for in next door
There is a cat that I like more
Than any other that I know;
Her name is Blanche, she's white as snow.

Now I am going to tell you why
I didn't enjoy last Christmas pie,
Explaining, first, Blanche had to wear—

Her mistress tied it with such care—
A ribbon blue, and I must say
She wore it in a graceful way.

My mistress saw it, and she said,
Zulu must wear a ribbon red;
His coat is black, he'll look as well
As Blanche in blue, with little bell.
And from that day, the ribbon bow
I had to wear; it brought me woe.
Oh, botheration! I did flare
Out on a bough, I hung in air.

I was below, and listening for
The tinkle of the bell she wore;
And listening for her timid mew,
The prettiest of the cats, I knew.
And this is how it happened, well,
Sometimes I heard her, and could tell
That she was close up to the wall,
In easy distance to my call.

Now let me your attention hold.
Out in the garden it was cold;
I had been sitting by the fire,
But to see Blanche was my desire.
I could not hear her, so I got
Impatient, and I jump'd the plot
For flowers, and I jump'd a tree—
Quite at the bottom there are three.

Heard nothing, so I tried the wall,
And then, somehow, I had a fall;
Where often I had jump'd before,
Now I shall do it nevermore.
Suspended from a bough I swung,
Entirely by the ribbon hung.

There on a twig it caught me, so
How I detest a ribbon bow;
A mercy that I was not killed.
My mistress saw it and was fill'd
With consternation.   Oh! she cried;
Look! from the window I have spied
My Zulu, hanging from a tree;
They all ran out to rescue me.

I was too high for them to reach;
You should have heard those people screech.
My Mistress pull'd me by the tail,
Which broke the knot, it was but frail.
My Mistress took me in; said she,
We'll give him something nice for tea.

'Twas Christmas Eve, so she was able
To hand me dainties from the table.
She tried me with some brandy first,
I would not take it; no, I nursed
My keen resentment for the bow.
I long pretended not to know—

That I had got a nice mince pie
Close under one unconscious eye.
She tried me with plum pudding hot.
I still lie there, too bad to spot
The things she put close by my nose.
How well the fire blaze warm'd my toes.

At last my Mistress, frightened quite,
Said, bad it's made his appetite.
Pray cut him off a little wing
From that big fowl, it will bring
Him round.   But now I would not eat
The fowl wing, too great a treat.

I went and hid it in the ground.
Next day I show'd it, safe and sound,
To Blanche—it was the kindest thing
My Mistress did—that fowl wing.
I quite forgave her for the tie
Of ribbon red that hung me high.

Enter Cupid.

    What can I be doing?
      Hanging mistletoe
   High up in the lobby,
     Where the folks all go.
  See, I leave my berries
     Swaying to and fro.

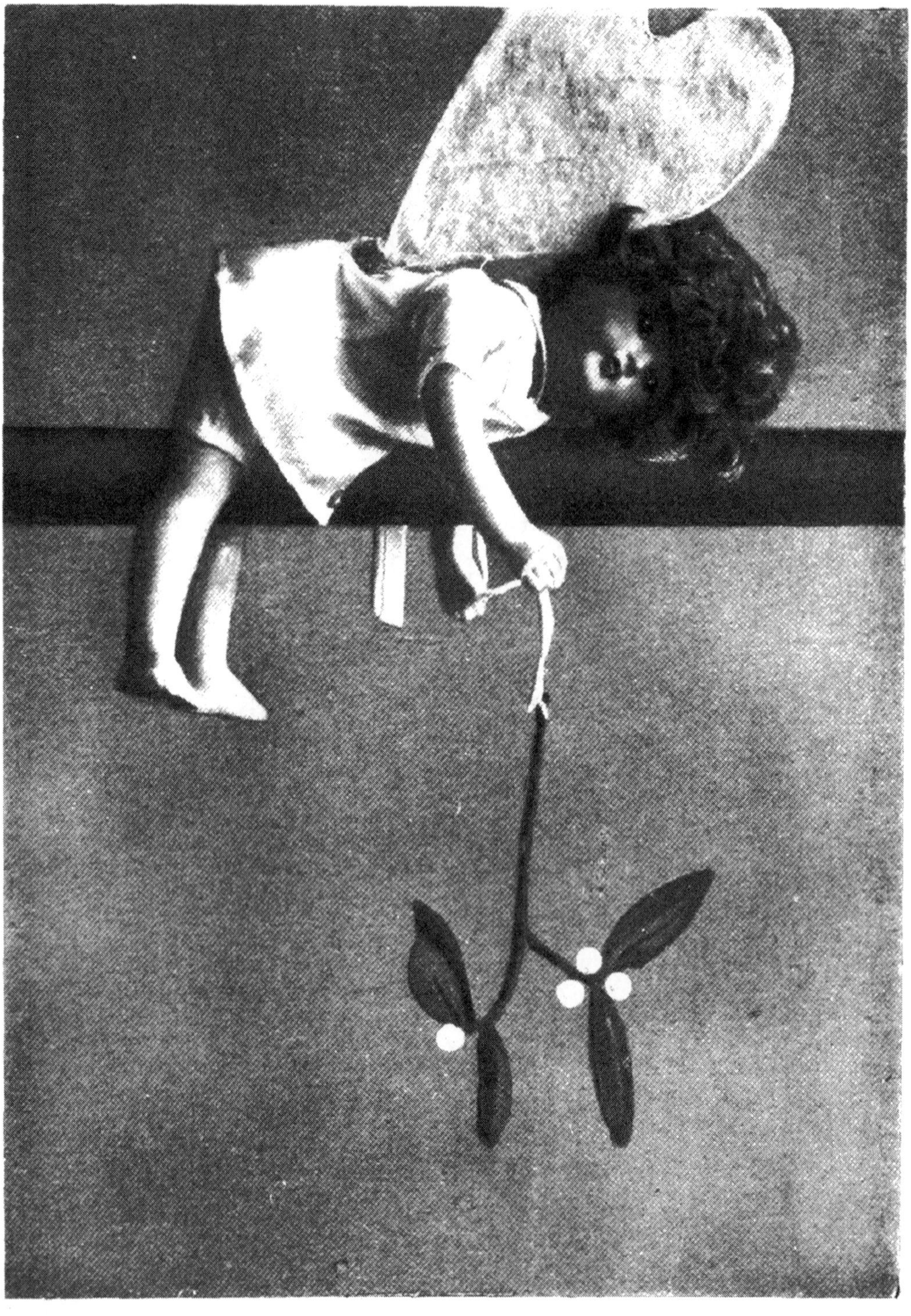

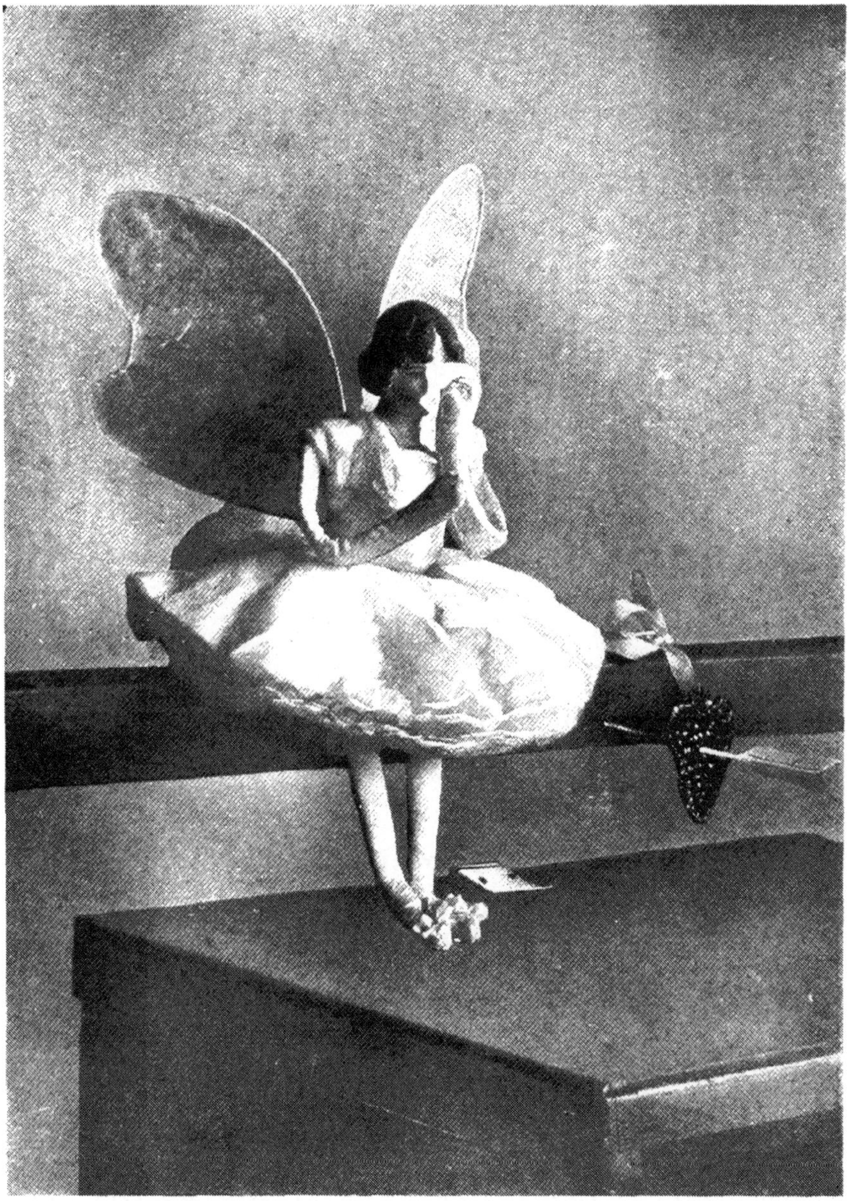

BRITISH
25 MAR 15

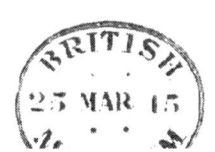

> What have I been doing?
>   To the fairy's heart;
> Put an arrow through it,
>   Just to make it smart.
> She can pull it out,
>   'Tis but a little dart.

Cupid, after hanging the mistletoe, hangs up the fairy's heart in a conspicuous place, but not too high for her to find it.

Enter Fairy Kindheart. *Seeing her heart thus she sinks into a chair sobbing into her handkerchief.* Cupid *points at* Kindheart *with great glee. While she sobs he shouts:*

> To find an arrow,
>   Tears begin to start;
> To find an arrow
>   Through her red, red heart.
> The Fairy's sorrow
>   Makes her weep like rain;
> Perhaps to-morrow
>   She will smile again.
> For she can wear it,
>   Now it has been found;
> The shot did tear it,
>   Let it be made sound.

Exeunt Cupid.

Kindheart *approaches her heart. After taking the arrow out she puts it on, not much the worse for* Cupid's *treatment. She sits down and awaits the coming of the others.*

Enter FLEETFOOT, *holding a long blue stocking.*

Enter MONEYBAGS, *holding a large bag with the word Money worked on it in large letters. They sit one on each side of* KINDHEART, *who is quite cheerful again.*

KINDHEART: What have you got there, Fleetfoot?
(*gaily*)   You are swaying to and fro;
                A funny rag, is it a flag
                   That you should wave it so?

FLEETFOOT: Why, Kindheart, can't you see it is
                A stocking that I sport?

KINDHEART: It cannot be a Scotchman's,
                For they always wear it short.

FLEETFOOT: I'm looking for a little girl
                Who mostly wears a sock;
               Now Christmas time she will be glad
                Of this fine lengthy stock.

KINDHEART: A Scotch child? And you, Moneybags,
                What is it you have got?
               You jingle like a wealthy bank;
                I hope you're worth a lot?

MONEYBAGS: At present I have only pence,
                They always make a noise;
               I'm collecting for the Widow's Fund,
                And orphans, girls and boys,

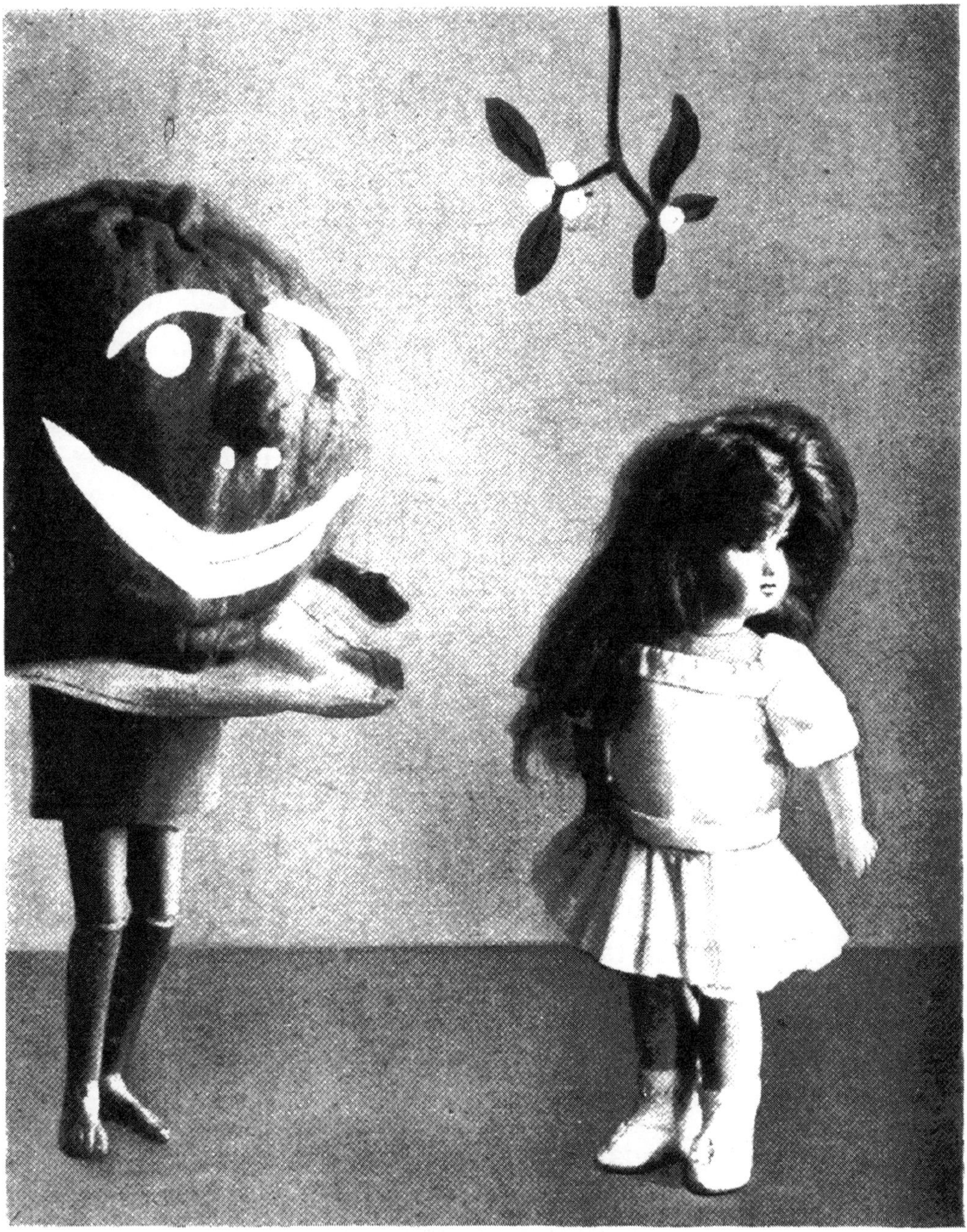

                    Whose husbands, fathers, in this war—
                        A noble hero band—
                    Have fallen on the battlefield,
                        To save our native land.

KINDHEART: I hope you'll be successful
                    And collect a goodish bit.
                Let us now be up and working,
                    We can't do much while we sit
                In lazy conversation.   Let us go,
                    We've said our say;
                I hope, dear Moneybags,
                    You will collect a lot to-day.

Exeunt.

Enter THE PUDDING—*he walks under the mistletoe.*

PUDDING: I'm going to stay under
                    This fine spray I've found.

GUINEA ONE: His face it is greasy
                    And grinny and round.
                He talks in a voice
                    That is pleasant and bold.

PUDDING: I fear it will snow,
                    For it blows up so cold.
                I wish you bright Christmas,
                    Come, kiss me, now do;
                I think it delightful here,
                    Only us two.

49

You shouldn't stand under
  The mistletoe there;
You don't want to kiss me,
  It's not at all fair.
Exeunt GUINEA ONE.

Enter CUPID:
I'll oblige you, say how many.

GUINEA ONE *enters, holding out her sock. She goes partly behind the scenes and knocks. Chorus behind the stage:*

Wake up, lend her
  A blue stocking, do;
Wake up, old dolls,
  You would if you knew
How outside your cupboard
  Door she knocks;
Come to tell you
  She only wears socks.
Wake up, old dolls,
  Now strike you a light;
Lend a stocking for
  Santa Claus night.

The GUINEA ONE *is seen again, but this time with a stocking.*

THE SUPPER TABLE.

CUPID:
Our supper table it is laid
With jelly, custard, lemonade;
And in the middle, crowning all,
Our handsome cake—so big and tall.
Now that we light the candles up,
Brave people all come in to sup.

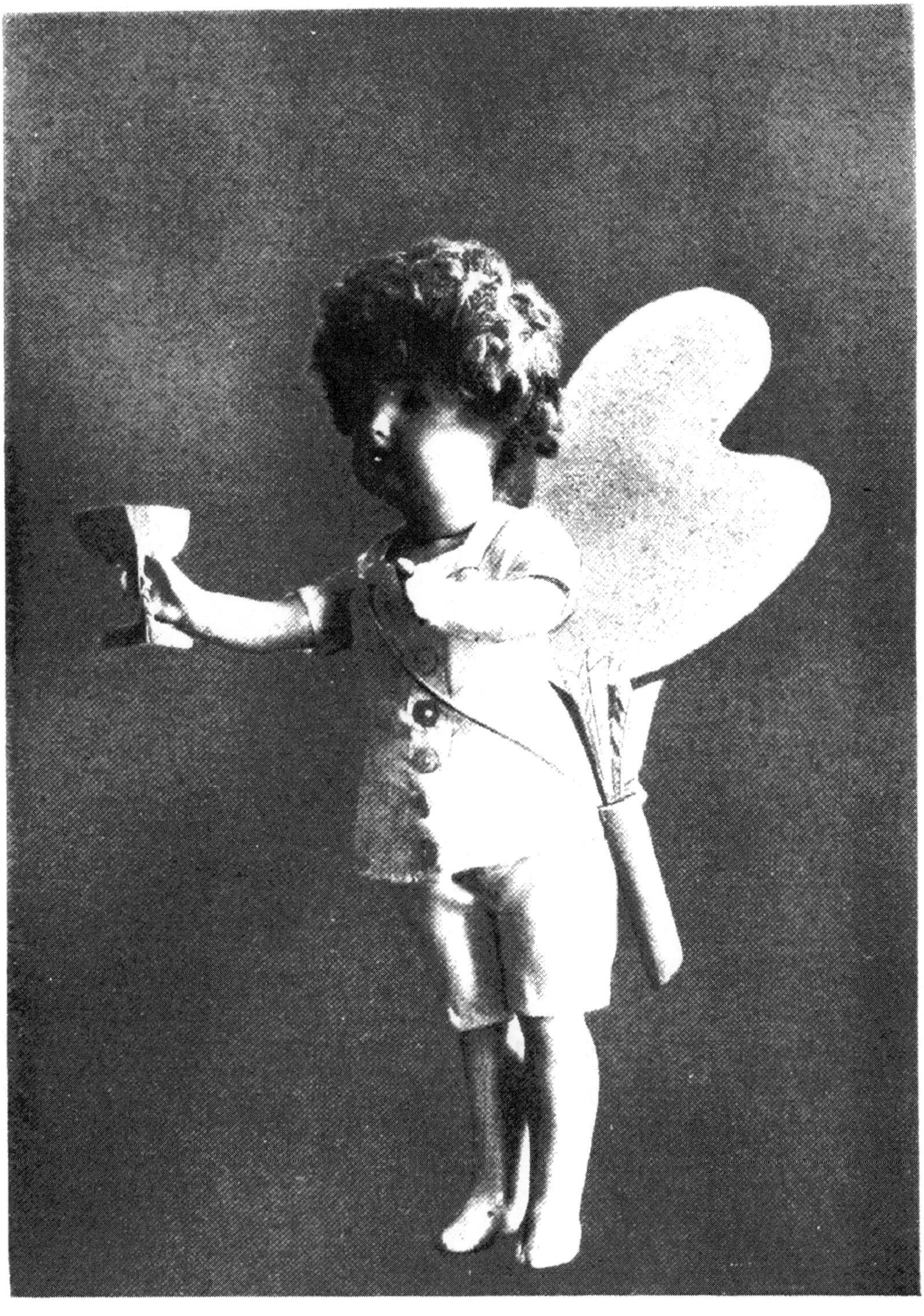

Here Cupid *lights the candles on and round the cake. All the characters come in except the* Guinea One.

Dame Trot: She was so tired, the small doll said,
She thought that she would go to bed.

Cupid: Come, look at me, I fill my glass;
I feel this evening cannot pass
Until a toast you all have drunk:
" The Guinea Doll and her fine trunk."

Kindheart: We must excuse the Guinea One to-night; she is anxious to be up early to-morrow. She is going to help us herself to make hospital shirts. At least she is going to make some sleeves, she says.

With three toy drums, three little British Boys sing The National Anthem.

THE END.

You can now get a book called " The National Anthems of the Allies," 9d. (Great Britain, France, Belgium, Russia, Japan), which would sound lovely for the three little boys to sing.

ARDEN PRESS LETCHWORTH

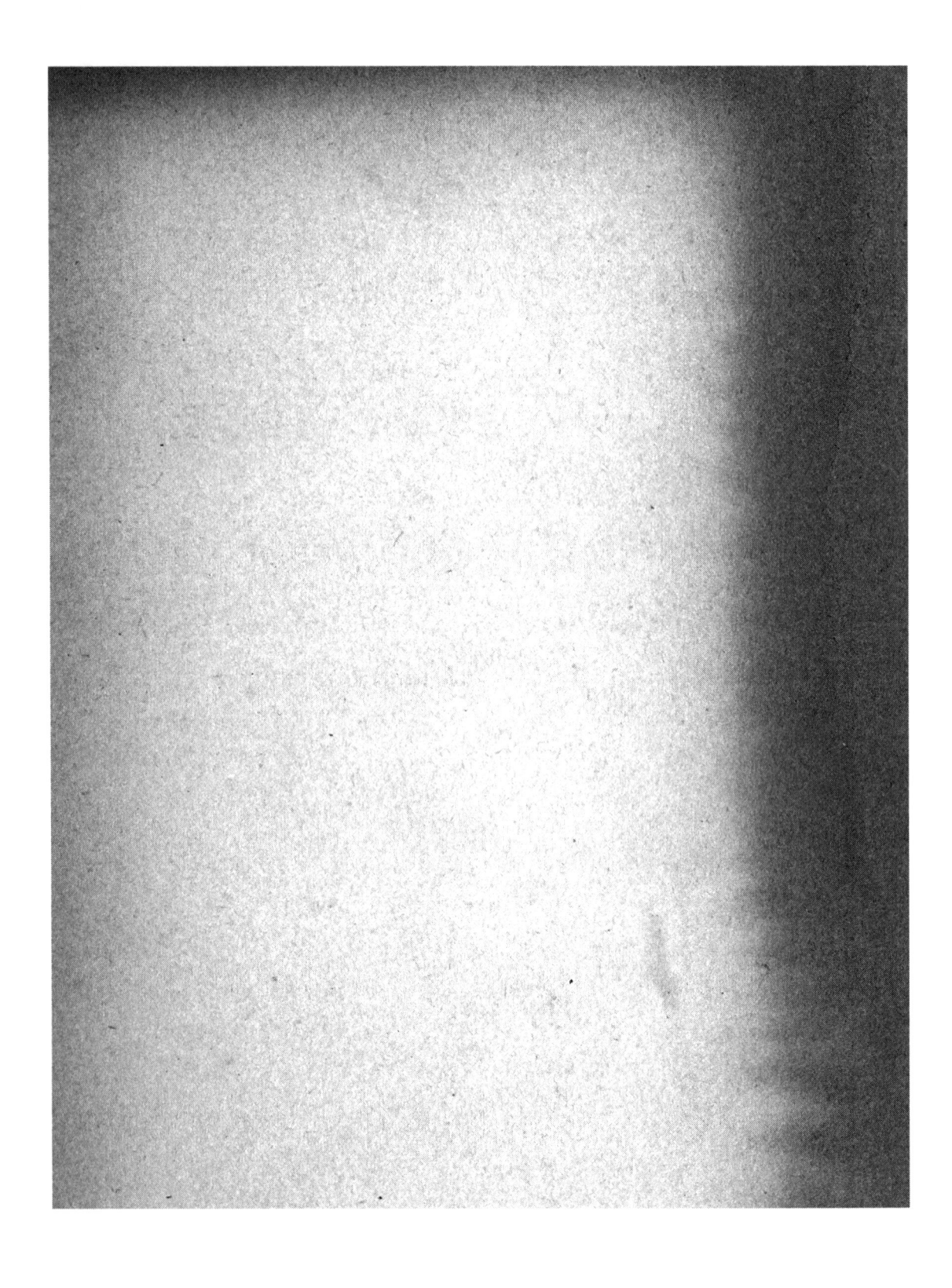

Lightning Source UK Ltd.
Milton Keynes UK
UKHW030702020120
356178UK00006B/158/P